ISBN 978-1-331-29041-4
PIBN 10169640

This book is a reproduction of an important historical work. Forgotten Books uses
state-of-the-art technology to digitally reconstruct the work, preserving the original format
whilst repairing imperfections present in the aged copy. In rare cases, an imperfection in
the original, such as a blemish or missing page, may be replicated in our edition. We do,
however, repair the vast majority of imperfections successfully; any imperfections that
remain are intentionally left to preserve the state of such historical works.

English
Français
Deutsche
Italiano
Español
Português

www.forgottenbooks.com

Mythology Photography **Fiction**
Fishing Christianity **Art** Cooking
Essays Buddhism Freemasonry
Medicine **Biology** Music **Ancient**
Egypt Evolution Carpentry Physics
Dance Geology **Mathematics** Fitness
Shakespeare **Folklore** Yoga Marketing
Confidence Immortality Biographies
Poetry **Psychology** Witchcraft
Electronics Chemistry History **Law**
Accounting **Philosophy** Anthropology
Alchemy Drama Quantum Mechanics
Atheism Sexual Health **Ancient History**
Entrepreneurship Languages Sport
Paleontology Needlework Islam
Metaphysics Investment Archaeology
Parenting Statistics Criminology
Motivational

MONT BLANC,

AND

Other Poems.

BY MARY ANN BROWNE,

IN HER FIFTEENTH YEAR.

Gleamings of poetry — if I may give
The name of beauty, passion, or of grace,
To the wild thoughts that, in a starlit hour,
In a pale twilight or a rosebud morn,
Glance o'er my spirit — thoughts that are like light,
Or love, or hope, in their effects.

L. E. L.

LONDON

HATCHARD AND SON, PICCADILLY; SEELEY, 169 FLEET
STREET; AND W. BENNING, 52 FLEET STREET.

1827.

TO

HER ROYAL HIGHNESS

THE PRINCESS AUGUSTA SOPHIA.

———

MADAM,

SHOULD these early efforts of my timid Muse succeed in obtaining the public approbation; the protection which YOUR ROYAL HIGHNESS has deigned to afford them will be my dearest honour; should they fail, my greatest consolation.

I have the honour to remain,

Madam,

Your Royal Highness's

Most Grateful and Faithful

Humble Servant,

MARY ANN BROWNE.

THE ELMS,
Maidenhead Thicket, Berks.

PREFACE.

A FRIEND of the Authoress is requested to write a preface, and feels himself in the situation of a daw that undertakes to introduce a nightingale.

Those who have asked him if the young lady has received no assistance, he has referred to the internal evidence afforded by these poems, convinced that the genius which they display is of too decided a character to derive advantage from extraneous aid; but as this answer may not satisfy all, he adds, that they are the entirely unassisted productions of the very young lady whose name they bear, and who has passed the few years of her life altogether in a state of country retirement, unacquainted with poets, except through their works, and guided by no other rules than her own feelings and imagination.

He would offer to these poems his tribute of praise; but it would want authority, and fall infinitely short of his opinion of their merit ; and after all the public must be the judge. He will not deprecate the critics, believing that a second will not be found who could, in the mere wantonness of flippant criticism, barbarously nip the early bud of genius and savagely exult in the destruction of the fair hopes and aspirations of youth.

ISLEWORTH,
March, 22, 1827.

CONTENTS.

	PAGE
MONT BLANC	3
On Reading an Assertion " That Woman was devoid of Sense, and that she never did any good without it was to lead to Evil."	11
On reading " Blacket's Remains."	14
The Withered Rose	15
My Harp	17
Written in an Album	19
On the Origin of the Red Rose	22
St. Mark's Eve : a Fragment	23
Stanzas	28
Tears	29
Loves	32
Hebrew Melody	36
Forget me not	38
Fragment	40

CONTENTS.

From a Wife to her Husband in Adversity 42

To my Sister ; with an Ivy Wreath on her Birth-Day.... 45

" Oh believe not, my Dearest." 47

To the Maid of Erin 49

Stanzas to Mary 51

To Mary on seeing her Portrait..................... 55

To Mrs. Hannah Moore 58

Stanzas 60

Yesterday 63

" I speak not of Beauty." 66

OCEAN 69

To my Grandmother on completing her Eightieth Year .. 77

" The last time I stood by this River." 79

" I saw thee in Light." 83

Friendship 85

Ennisfall 87

Stanzas on the Death of a young Lady 91

Friendship and Love............................... 94

Song 96

The Mourner to New-Year's Day.................... 97

" They may talk of their Flowers." 100

Lament for a Highland Chieftain 101

" Farewell, thou False One." 104

Stanzas 106

Greece : Affectionately inscribed to C. T. Robertson, Esq.. 109

" To-Morrow, Dear departed one" 113

Verses, written after reading the Anacreontic Song in
   " The Light of the Haram" in Moore's " Lallah Rookh." 116

The Maniac 119

She Dreameth 122

Disappointment 126

The Recluse to the World........................... 128

Stanzas 131

The Ivy in Winter.................................. 134

" I saw in the Evening" 136

THE VALLEY OF ROSES 139

SACRED PIECES.

The Sabbath 161

To the Jessamine 165

" I heard her Pray" 166

Stanzas written in the Author's Bible the Day she com-
   pleted her Fourteenth Year 170

The Tear 172

" Watch and Pray" 174

MONT BLANC,

&c.

MONT BLANC.

Around his waist are forests braced,
And an avalanche in his hand.

*   *   *

It was the cooling hour, just when the rounded
Red sun sinks down behind the azure hill.

LORD BYRON.

MONARCH of mountains! in thy cloudy robe,

Thou sit'st secure upon thy craggy throne,

Seeming to lord it over half the globe,

As if the world beneath were all thine own : —

Encircled with thy pure, thine icy zone,

Thou lift'st towards heaven thy proud majestic breast ;

Above this nether world thou stand'st alone,

And seem'st to dare the sun to touch thy vest ;

Thou laugh'st and shak'st the storm from thy tremendous crest.

Thy cataract, rushing on with madd'ning force,

Leaps in its sport along thy fertile base : —

No human eye can search its mighty source —

No human thought its origin can trace —

They can but see it rush into the vase

Heaven hath assign'd it in the vale below —

They can but see it foam its desperate race

Amidst the scatter'd avalanche of snow

That thou hast shorn and thrown from thine exalted brow.

The sun is setting, — and his parting beams

Their own pure beauties o'er thy bosom shed,

And light clouds float around thee, like the dreams

That wave their pinions o'er the sleeper's bed ;

And round thy form so desolate and dread

A flood of soft and rosy sun-light plays,

And brightness o'er thy snowy breast is spread,

Like memory revelling in past pleasure's blaze,

Or calling back the calm of other happier days.

Faster and faster sinks the setting sun, —

And now he reaches the horizon's verge ;

His task is o'er, his daily race is run,

His flaming steeds their course no longer urge ;

And now, like the low dash of distant surge,

The evening breezes sing their nightly song,

Solemn and low, as floats a funeral dirge ;

The night-wind and its echoes creep along,

And the pines rustle that they walk their way among.

'Tis night, — and all is silent, all is dark —

No light is seen, and not a sound is heard,

Save 'tis a shepherd watchdog's distant bark,

Or the short twitter of some startled bird,

Until, as if by some enchanter stirr'd,

The moon slow rises in her bright array,

As, in obedience to the wizard word,

She came to chase the awful dark away,

And smile the night into a sweeter softer day.

Short is her reign ; — for o'er thee broods a storm

That wraps in darkness thy stupendous height;

Its circling clouds are gathering round thy form ;

Onward it comes in awful gloomy state,

In its dun bosom bears its fatal freight,

And o'er all nature spreads its pall of black,

And, as it flies, it seems to gather weight,

Till, in the madness of its desperate track,

It seems to seize the moon and hurl her struggling back.

The thunder bursts in one tremendous crash —

The lightning quivering leaps from rock to rock —

Peal answering peal, and flash succeeding flash ;

While thousand echoes each new valley mock,

Till nature, rous'd by the electric shock,

Sends forth her groans to swell the dreadful choir ;

And now the clouds their prison'd stores unlock,

And pour their torrents forth to quench the fire

That else might melt the earth in its too furious ire.

The storm is nearly o'er — the tempest clears —
The lightnings distant and more distant stream, —
The moon amidst the pris'ning clouds appears,
And looks forth with a trembling troubled beam ;
And now the lightnings cease their baleful gleam,
The tempest sinks away to its abyss,
And she once more resumes her silver dream,
And pours upon the earth a shower of bliss,
And nature meets her soft, her reconciling kiss.

Amidst these changes, *thou* hast stood unchanged ;
And haply shalt for many a coming age.
Thou risest o'er the mountains round thee ranged,
As independent; and the tempest's rage
Cannot destroy thee; and thou oft shalt wage
War with the elements while time shall be, —
The wonder of the poet and the sage, —
Till that day come, when heaven and earth shall flee,
And in the general wreck o'erwhelm thee — even thee.

Mountain of mountains ! thy stupendous height,

On which the moon-beams now so softly shine,

Must bow before the Lord of power and might,

Must quake if touched by the hand divine ;

Wrench'd from thy seat by mightier power than thine,

Hurl'd from thy throne of rocks, then even thou

Must all thy stedfast dignity resign ;

And, headlong thrown, e'en thy gigantic brow

Must kiss the earth thou frownest proudly over now.

I turn to leave thee, King of thousand hills !

Lord of the valley that beneath thee lies !

I turn to leave thee and thy frozen rills,

Where the soft gentian opes its wild blue eyes ;—

I leave thee, canopied beneath the skies,

And folded in thy robe of ermine snows ;

And when thou tak'st again the veil of dyes

The parting glance of day-light o'er thee throws,

I shall be far from thee and all thy tints of rose.

Thy fast-receding summit seems a pile

Of light clouds, resting 'gainst the summer sky,

Brighten'd by the soft moon-beams' gentle smile

That lights around thy fleecy drapery ;

And on thy diadem, the forests lie,

Seeming but emeralds in thy crystal crown ;

While, for a moment hanging awfully

Upon thy crest, as if it stopp'd to frown

Upon the scene beneath, the av'lanche totters down.

My lay is ended,—but my hand still lingers

Upon my harp, however harsh its tone ;

And once again must my untutor'd fingers

Sweep o'er the chords I still may call my own.

Oh ! be the parting accents o'er thee thrown,

And be thy valley with their echoes filled !

Oh ! may they pierce thro' e'en thy snowy zone,

And reach thee, as they leave my heart, unchill'd,

And thro' th' electric chain of linking mountains thrill'd !

May'st thou long lift aloft thy snowy crest

Pure and unruffled, as I leave it now ;

May calm long settle on thy peaceful breast,

And sweetest sun-light float around thy brow ;

And may the summer sun-set's ruddy glow

Throw its soft influence round thee like a spell ;

May thy blue gentians still upon thee blow,

And poets of thy wondrous beauties tell !

Monarch of rocks and hills ! for ever fare thee well !

ON READING AN ASSERTION

"THAT WOMAN WAS DEVOID OF SENSE, AND THAT SHE NEVER
DID ANY GOOD WITHOUT IT WAS TO LEAD TO EVIL."

Oh, why say that Woman is faithless and light,

And that wisdom alone to thy sex is confined;

That her heart is as false as her beauty is bright,

And her loveliness lies in her face — not her mind?

Remember, 'twas Woman first lull'd thee to rest;

Remember, 'twas she that first over thee hung, —

That thou slept'st thy first sleep on a Woman's fond breast,

And thy first infant accents were caught from her tongue.

She guided thy steps in thy infantine years —

    She anxiously watch'd where thy careless feet stray'd —

She hush'd all thy wailing — she dried all thy tears —

    And delighted she saw thy young genius display'd.

And is not fair Woman the sweet'ner of life?

    With man she divides her enjoyments and cares, —

The Friend or the Sister, the Daughter or Wife, —

    Alike in his pleasure or sorrow she shares.

She is like the fair woodbine that wreathes round the oak,

    That derives its support from the tree's noble stem ;

And, tho' it be scathed by the lightning's dread stroke,

    Still weaves of its flowrets a rich diadem.

'Tis Woman supports and consoles man's decline —

    She drops o'er his woes the pure pitying tear,

And her love, like a tendril, still round him will twine,

    A tendril that Time cannot wither or sear.

'Tis she who will watch the last life-drop depart

   From the cheek, where so often her smile has removed

The dark cloud,—then will feel the last throb of the heart,

   And weep o'er the corse of the being she loved.

She will freely confess she is weaker than thee ;

   But her weakness should move not thine anger, but love:

Oh, thou should'st remember those moments, when she

   Hath cheer'd thee, and seem'd like a form from above.

To thee for instruction and strength she must cling,

   For she does not pretend to be wise as thou art ;

Her impulses flow from affection's warm spring,

   Her feelings are not from the head, but the heart.

Then why say she only by malice is stirr'd ?

   No! even her failings from kindness descend :—

Oh, revoke the rude sentence — recall the harsh word,

   And Woman henceforth shall be ever thy friend.

ON READING "BLACKET'S REMAINS."

Martyr to genius ! rude misfortune's blast
Oft sear'd thee, as thy lowly cot it pass'd ;—
The threatening tempests darkly o'er thee gloom'd,
And strove to crush the bud, ere yet it bloom'd ;—
And, tho' sweet comfort's soul-reviving rays
Shone out to cheer thee in thy latter days,
They were but as the sun-beams smiling o'er
The shatter'd bark they cannot bring to shore ;
Like some light cloud above the thirsty fields,
Dropping the treasures that its bosom yields,
Dispensing all its store of balmy tears,
Until it fades away and disappears ;
So were thy talents in thy life's short day,
Till, like that cloud, they wept themselves away.

THE WITHERED ROSE.

I saw, at eve, a wither'd rose —
    The sun's warm ray had curl'd it ;
Its powerless leaves it could not close,
    And dewy tears impearl'd it :

I saw a moon-beam gently rest —
    The withered flower it lighten'd ;
And though it could not dry its breast,
    Those crystal drops it brighten'd.

I looked again — that moon-beam fair
    Had gilded o'er its weeping,
And that sweet flow'ret calmly there
    Beneath its ray was sleeping.

So when Misfortune's night-blast sears,

    Fair Friendship's smile we borrow ;

And, tho' it cannot dry our tears,

    'Twill chase the gloom of sorrow.

MY HARP.

My Harp had long hung on a withering tree, —
  The snow lay around it, and loud howl'd the blast;
It had not been touch'd since I touch'd it for thee,
  And the winter wind sigh'd thro' its strings as it pass'd.

No lay to its soft flowing tones had been sung, —
  No hand had awaken'd its heavenly strain,
Till the last leaf that fell from the oak where it hung,
  Touch'd one of its strings and arous'd it again.

And the tones of that harp just as lovelily thrill'd,
  As if touch'd by the fingers of beauty once more;
And the air with harmonious music it fill'd,
  Till it sank in the silence that bound it before.

So 'twas with my heart, — for it long had been bound

    In silence and misery, darkness and woe, —

And the storm-blast of sorrow was howling around,

    And my mind was congeal'd with adversity's snow.

Till a friendly voice whisper'd a once belov'd name,

    And my heart leap'd for joy at the sweet soothing words;

And the mem'ry of love fill'd my soul with its flame,

    And drew forth sweet tones from the long-silent chords.

And for one little moment my dream was renew'd,

    And my soul with the joy of remembrance burn'd,

Till the sounds into silence again were subdued,

    And my heart to its desolate darkness return'd.

WRITTEN IN AN ALBUM.

Unworthy though I am to claim
  Remembrance fond of one like thee,
Yet on this page I trace my name,
  That thou may'st sometimes think of me.

Tho' many, worthier far, have placed
  The tributes of their Friendship here,
Thou wilt not deem the page disgraced
  By one who holds thee very dear.

'Midst many a gay and splendid flower,
  The Violet sweetness still can breathe ; —
And thus be this, tho' slight its power,
  The Violet in Affection's wreath.

Mary ! I soon shall be afar ; —
    Perhaps this meeting is our last ;
But be our love like evening's star,
    Smiling when life's bright day is past.

And when my life has pass'd its prime,
    Then will dear thoughts of thine and thee
Come floating on the waves of time,
    Like flowers thrown o'er a troubled sea.

'Tis well that I should write this now ; —
    What might it be in future years ?
Then I, how'd down by earthly woe,
    Might stain the spotless page with tears.

And these weak lines, that are but now
    Affection's tribute ere we part,
Might then, wrung forth by sorrow, flow —
    The life-drops from a bleeding heart.

But we will turn from such sad themes,

    And fly to those more fit for youth,

Although they be but morning dreams

    To fade before the light of truth.

Then thou wilt not this lay despise ; —

    Here thou in future years may'st see

My name ; — and when it meets thine eyes,

    Mary ! thou wilt remember me !

IMPROMPTU

ON THE ORIGIN OF THE RED ROSE.

The Rose that blooms in blushing crimson bright,
As Poets' legends tell us, once was white:
It turn'd its modest face towards the sky,
Pure and unstain'd by any earthly dye;
It ceas'd that spotless look to heaven to raise,
And downwards on a streamlet fix'd its gaze;
It saw its ivory petals mirror'd there,
And blush'd to see itself so very fair;
The consciousness of beauty changed its hue,
And the *white* Rose the lovely *red* one grew.

ST. MARK'S EVE, *

A FRAGMENT.

—————

Now it is the time of night,
　　That the graves, all gaping wide,
Every one lets forth his spright,
　　In the church-way paths to glide.

MIDSUMMER-NIGHT'S DREAM.

—————

The Ladye stood by the ruin'd arch,

　　And listed the sound of the breeze,

As it whistled along the mouldering wall,

　　Or murmur'd amid'st the trees.

—————

* For a particular account of this superstition, see " Bracebridge Hall;" by the Author of the " Sketch Book." page 99, vol. 1.

'Twas the Eve of St. Mark, and she stood by the church,
  And gazed with undaunted eye
On the ruin'd form of the ancient porch,
  To mark what shades would pass by.

Twice before had she tried the spell,
  And twice had she said the prayer ;
And now, the third and decisive time,.
  That Ladye was watching there.

For whoever will watch on the Eve of St. Mark,
  Without a tremble or fear,
Shall see the forms pass thro' the church porch,
  Of those who shall die in that year.

The moon was rising above the hill,
  And her soft beam pensively smil'd,
And she look'd o'er the world that lay sleeping below,
  Like a mother that hangs o'er her child.

The distant dog howl'd long and loud,

And shrilly whistled the blast,

And the Ladye stedfastly look'd around,

To mark each omen that pass'd.

Pale was her cheek in the pale moon-light,

And her lily brow lay bare,

And many a jewel and many a gem

Was sparkling amid'st her hair.

A light cloud rose in the Heaven's blue vault,

And the night-breezes bore it along,

And carried it wrapp'd in their viewless arms,

And sang it their evening song.

And they placed it before the pale moon-beams,

And it rested a moment there,

Like the fair lamp of brightest love,

Blotted by clouds of care.

The cloud pass'd away, and the moon again
   Shone on the ivy-wrapt tower;
And the wind died away to a murmuring moan,
   And the clock toll'd the midnight hour.

The chill dew fell on the Ladye's brow,
   As she sat on a broken stone,
And she whisper'd again the midnight spell,
   And she fear'd not to sit there alone.

The Ladye turu'd and look'd on the church,
   And as she gazed on that pile,
A rushing sound like the night-blast swept
   Along the ruin'd aisle —

     *   *   *

       *   *   *

* * * * * *

* * * * *

Not mine to tell what tale she heard,

   Or to open the scroll of fate ;

But the Ladye was found at the blush of the morn,

   A clay-cold corpse at the gate.

STANZAS.

Lay me not 'neath a stately pile,
  Proudly 'mid others rising;
Bury me not in the fretted vault;—
  They are below my prizing:—
But carry me to the grass-grown grave,
  Where *she* is sleeping before me;
And let that grave with flowers be strown,
  And a willow waving o'er me.

Let no storied marble tell
  Of the dust that lies beneath it;
Let no sculptur'd mourner be there,
  Nor chissell'd garland enwreath it;
But plant it with flowers of fleeting bloom,
  As the fittest and fairest token,
To tell the pensive passer-by
  The heart that lies there was broken.

TEARS.

———

The tear most sacred — shed for others pain,
That starts at once — bright — pure — from pity's mine,
Already polish'd by the hand divine !

Lord Byron.

———

What is that tear — that sorrowless tear —

   That rests on the infant's cheek awhile,

'Till the fond parent coming near

   Soon chases away the drop by her smile ? —

'Tis the morning dew upon the flower,

   Whose leaves awhile may the gem retain,

'Till the sun-beam at its rising hour

   Will dry the lovely blossom again.

What is that beautiful crystal that flows
    Down the yet unfurrow'd, tho' weeping cheek ;
The tear that is shed for another's woes,
    That peace to the sorrowing heart can speak ? —
'Tis the dew that gently falls to earth
    In the gloom of night and the twilight of eve,
That calls new buds and blossoms forth,
    And refreshes the feverish earth beneath.

What are those drops that heavily roll
    From the eye to which weeping hath long been denied,
That ease the grief of the woe-laden soul,
    As if half its sorrow away it had sigh'd ? —
'Tis the shower that falls from the dark heavy cloud
    That long had obscured the bright bosom of day,
And, reliev'd from its sadd'ning, dark'ning load,
    The sun's smiling beam will soon chase it away.

What are those tears — those penitent tears —
    That dim the contrite sinner's eye,
That calm the guilty's rising fears,
    And reach the throne of Mercy on high ? —

They are the cooling torrents that dash,

   When the thunder peal is rolling above,—

That quench the lightnings angry flash,

   As tears the heavenly mercy move.

What is that gem that falls on the bed,

   Where the dying saint is breathing his last,

Who brightness around him still can shed,

   And a parting smile on that tear-drop cast?—

'Tis the dewy balm of the summer's night,

   As it weeps for the sun when 'tis sinking to rest,

Which throws a ray of parting light

   To illumine that dew-drop's crystal breast.

LOVES.

Love rules the court, the camp, the grove,
And men below, and Saints above ;
For love is Heaven, and Heaven is love.

SCOTT.

There is a love by Nature fix'd,

Deep planted in the human heart ;

It is a feeling pure — unmix'd —

That cannot from the breast depart.

It is the love the mother bears

To the sweet babe she lulls to rest —

The object of her tenderest cares —

The fondest thought that warms her breast.

There is a love, so fond, so true,

    No art the magic tie can sever;—

'Tis ever beauteous, ever new,—

    Its chain, once link'd, is link'd for ever.

It is the first delightful thrill

    That dawns within the maiden's heart,

That Time's cold wing can never chill,

    Or force its silver tie apart.

There is a love, a passionate beam,

    Too fond, too warm, too bright to last,—

The frenzy of a fever'd dream,

    That burns a moment — then is past.

'Tis like the lightning's lurid glare,

    That streams its blaze of fatal light —

Flames for an instant thro' the air,—

    Then sinks away in deepest night.

D

There is a love, whose feeling rolls
  In pure unruffled calmness on,
The meeting of congenial souls,
  Of hearts whose currents flow in one.

It is a blessing that is felt
  But by united minds that flow,
As sun-beams into sun-beams melt,
  To light a frozen world below.

There is a love, that o'er the war
  Of jarring passions pours its light —
And sheds its influence, like the star
  That brightest burns in darkest night.

It is a love but known to those
  Who, hand in hand, amidst the strife,
Together have withstood their foes,
  Together shared the storms of life.

It is so true, so fix'd, so strong,

   It parts not with the parting breath ;

In the soul's flight 'tis borne along,

   And holds the heart-strings, e'en in death.

'Tis never quench'd by sorrow's tide ; —

   No ! tis a flame caught from above, —

A tie that death cannot divide

   'Tis the bright torch of wedded love.

But there is one love, not of earth,

   Tho' sullied by the streaming tear ; —

It is a star of heavenly birth,

   And only shines unshaken *there*.

'Tis when this clay resigns its breath,

   And the soul quits its frail abode, —

That, rising from the bed of death,

   This love is pure — the love of God.

HEBREW MELODY.

I saw thy raven hair
   Bound by a jewell'd band,
And many a circlet fair
   Was on thy beauteous hand,
And a bright chain of Ophir's gold
Was round that neck of Phidian mould.

I saw those tresses twine
   Around thy forehead even ;
I saw thy dark eyes shine
   As blaze the stars in heaven ;
I gazed upon thy bosom fair
And not one thorn, one grief was there.

I saw that bosom's snow
   Stain'd by the crimson gore;
I heard that voice in woe,
   That sang so sweet before:
I saw thy raven tresses torn;
I heard thee made the ruffian's scorn.

I saw those beauties sold
   To heed the Assyrian's beck,
And for thy chain of gold,
   Was iron round thy neck;
But tho' they might to slavery send,
Thy lofty soul they could not bend.

No; they who were thy Lords
   Might sharpen sorrow's dart,
And they might tear the chords
   That bound thy noble heart;
But unto them it was not given
To keep thy soul from finding heaven.

FORGET ME NOT.

Farewell! farewell! my ever dear!
   Although to part must be our lot; —
Oh wipe away the starting tear,
   And think of the Forget-me-not!

Last night we sat in yonder bower —
   We walk'd beside that lowly grot —
We pluck'd a lovely simple flower,
   The brilliant blue Forget-me-not.

And when in distant lands I roam,
   Far from this dear and hallow'd spot,
And exile from my native home,
   Oh! think of the Forget-me-not.

When I return in happier hour,

    And visit thy beloved cot,

Again we'll walk and pluck that flower,

    The Lover's flower — Forget-me-not.

FRAGMENT.

I walk'd in the morn, when the beautiful shower
Had left its tears on many a flower,
When many a pearly diadem
Was hanging upon the rose's stem,
And the fair lily's bell was set
With a bright dewy coronet;
And there the jessamine was budding,
With silver stars its leaves bestudding,
And one rain-drop of lustre meek
Was laid on a rose's smiling cheek;
And the rising sun with its welcome glance
Had waked the buds from their evening trance,
And the ivy that circled the mouldering stone
Shone with a brilliancy not its own;
Flowers with nature's tears bedew'd,
That the pencil of heaven itself had blued,

Thro' their covert of green leaves flash,

Like a tearful eye thro' its long dark lash ;

The sun-beam dries the gentle showers,

And refresh'd are the beautiful smiling flowers.

And this is like the sorrowing mind : —

Grief often leaves a balm behind ;

And so on earth the soul appears

Refresh'd by salutary tears ;

And even if sorrow through life should remain,

We shall meet with peace in heaven again ;

And every tear of dark distress

Shall be dried by the Sun of Righteousness.

FROM A WIFE TO HER HUSBAND IN ADVERSITY.

Why heave that sigh, my only love ?
   Is, then, the scene so sad before thee,
That nothing can the thoughts remove
   That spread their dark'ning influence o'er thee ?

Believe me, thou art still as dear
   As when thou wast in wealth and riches ;
Oh, wipe away that starting tear ; —
   It is — it is thy wife beseeches !

Oh think upon those early days,
   When thou to strains I sung would'st listen ;
When thy fond look was my best praise,
   And with sweet tears thine eyes would glisten.

Believe me, love, 'tis still the same,

 The fruit is here, tho' fall'n the blossom : —

Time tempers, but not cools the flame

 That burns within the faithful bosom.

There is a thought may still beguile —

 . In joy or grief we've never parted. —

Oh, if I could but see thee smile,

 I should not be quite broken-hearted !

Oh, cease to heave the struggling sigh !

 Oh, dash away that tear, my dearest !

Believe me, happier days are nigh ; —

 When night is darkest, dawn is nearest ;

Look on our infant's artless wile,

 That strives to chase away thy sorrow ;

Canst thou not from that babe's sweet smile,

 One ray of joy to cheer thee borrow.

There is a something in my breast,

    That says we are not quite forsaken,—

That says once more we shall be blest,

    And joy's soft tone again shall waken.

Perchance the parting beam of life

    Will shed a peaceful sunshine o'er us;

Then hand in hand we'll quit the strife,

    With a bright thornless path before us.

TO MY SISTER,

WITH AN IVY WREATH, ON HER BIRTH-DAY,

Sept. 25th 1826.

Another year hath roll'd away;
  Summer gives place to Autumn's gloom,
And lengthen'd night and shorten'd day
  Proclaim my sister's birthday come.

Then, Martha, while thine hand receives
  The wreaths that mine for thee hath twin'd,
Read in their dark-green shining leaves
  A useful lesson to thy mind.

Virtue, like them, is ever green,
  Like them, fresh graces can impart,
Enlivening the gloomiest scene,
  And lightening the heaviest heart.

That ivy deck'd its parent tree,
  On whose young bosom it was born;
And so shall virtue be to thee,
  Gracing thy life's fair opening morn.

In later times it still shall twine,
  Encircling its native stem;
It shall support thy life's decline, —
  Its leaves thy emerald diadem.

'Twill guide thee in the way of love,
  'Twill grace thee when those locks are snow;
And in the blessed realms above,
  'Twill be the crown to bind thy brow.

" OH BELIEVE NOT, MY DEAREST."

Oh, believe not, my dearest, I ever could leave thee,

   Or cause thee to weep when life sinks in decay ;

Oh, think not, my love, that I e'er could deceive thee : —

   The sun brightest beams at the closing of day.

As the ivy encircles the ruin'd old cloister,

   And clings all the closer the nearer its end ;

So thee in my arms, love, I fondly will foster,

   And still prove myself thine unchangeable friend.

Oh, believe not, my love, when thine head is grown hoary,

   I'll leave thee for those in the bloom of their youth ;

The snow of the locks is a bright crown of glory,

   When found in the way of the sun-beam of truth.

But believe that I'll love and most fondly will cherish,

   And, as time steals upon us, but more will adore;

As roses scent sweetest when nearest to perish,

   My passion more fragrant shall burn than before.

TO THE MAID OF ERIN.

Oh Maid of Erin! do not weep,
    Or heave for me one sigh ;
But let the precious tear-drop sleep
    Within thy gentle eye.

Oh keep it in thine eye of blue ; —
    Resume thy self-command,
Till thy soft sigh shall waft the dew
    To thine own emerald land.

Alas ! too late ; — the little gem
    Falls o'er a rose-bud fair,
And, pendant on the flow'ret's stem,
    It hangs, and glitters there.

As the bright sun recalls the rain
  Back to its native heaven,
And in soft dew the show'r again
  To thirstier fields is given : —

So, Maid of Erin, by thy smile
  The fallen tear reclaim,
And for thine own, thy suffering isle,
  Oh! weep it o'er again.

STANZAS TO MARY.

Nay;— do not strive to check my tears,
　But let them flow unheeded on; —
The cherish'd hope of future years,
　The being I adored is gone.

Oh Mary! can it really be,
　Thy form relentless death hath struck; —
Were there no flowers less fair than thee,
　For his unsparing hand to pluck?

Must that fond cheek no longer glow
　With smiles to chase away my gloom?
Must that angelic form lie low,
　And wither in the silent tomb?

Thou wast a being moulded of

    All that the heart of man reveres, —

A form too fair for human love —

    An eye too bright for human tears.

I was in sorrow and disgrace : —

    To share them thou did'st not repine ; —

And if a smile illumed my face,

    'Twas but reflected there from thine.

Yes ; — in adversity, to me

    Thou clung'st with more than woman's love : —

Oh ! 'twas scarce sin to worship thee,

    Thou wast so like a saint above !

Thou wast so pure, that thou would'st not

    Believe that others were less free

From sin, — and scarce beheld the blot

    All other eyes could trace in me.

Oh could I e'er have lov'd thee less,

    Grief had not quite o'ercome my heart ; —

Had'st thou another liv'd to bless,

    Then anger might have claim'd a part.

But oh ! I could not brook to think

    That thou and all thy gentle charms

Must into cold oblivion sink,

    And moulder in death's ruthless arms.

But yet — perchance — 'twas well that thou

    Should'st fall ere age and earthly care

Had cast their shadows o'er thy brow,

    Or sorrow traced one wrinkle there.

Perhaps 'twas well that thou should'st die,

    Ere sin and shame were known to thee ;

Ere tears had dimm'd thy deep blue eye,

    Except 'twere those that flow'd for me, —

Ere thorns beset thy earthly lot,

    And bid thee at thy fate repine, —

Ere to thine eyes life seem'd a blot,

    As now its prospects are to mine.

Yes ! — thou art happy, and I wrong'd

    Thy spirit when I shed a tear :

My selfish heart had almost long'd

    To call thee from thy blessed sphere.

Submission is but vainly taught

    To hearts the fiend Despair has riven ;

And every pure and hallow'd thought

    Of mine has fled with thee to heaven.

TO MARY,

ON SEEING HER PORTRAIT.

Oh take that portrait from my sight; —
  I cannot bear to gaze
On eyes that only mock the light
  Hers shed on happier days.
And smiles so sweet — so like her own —
That I should think the living one
  Was shedding there its rays;
And I should cherish the dear thought
'Till I awoke and found her not.

My Mary ! does thy blessed soul
   Inhabit some bright sphere ?
Or does it roam from pole to pole,
   Or is it lingering near ?
Perhaps, e'en while I vainly weep,
Thy spirit guarding watch may keep
   O'er him who once was dear ; —
Once! my fair guardian Angel ; — thou
May'st well retain thine office *now ;* —

For ne'er before did spirit need
   So much a spirit's care ;
And ne'er did human heart yet bleed
   For one so young and fair.
Oh ! in mine anguish, succour me, —
If from thy bless'd Eternity
   One moment thou can'st spare : —
'Twill not be long —'twill soon be past —
Despair can not for ever last !

I shall not soon forget the smile

   Upon thy patient face,

When I was by, — tho' death the while

   There fix'd his dwelling-place ;

The eye that beam'd when I was near, —

But ah ! so faintly, that a tear

   Had lent it better grace ;

And those fond lips that, tho' in pain,

Refused to murmur or complain.

Oh Spirit ! if thou hast the power

   To temper my distress,

If thou can'st lighten this dark hour

   From thoughts of bitterness,

Look from thy radiant sphere above,

And cheer the object of thy love ; —

   Thy joy will not be less :

Then, my short life of sorrow o'er,

Mary ! we'll meet — to part no more.

TO MRS. HANNAH MORE.

Many daughters have done virtuously, but thou excellest them all.

Prov. xxxi. 29.

The Virtues a garland of praises were twining,

   And many a favourite name had call'd o'er,

When they hail'd one that purer and brighter was shining, —

   And they placed the blest wreath on the brows of our More.

Hail, glorious woman ! The sweet chord of feeling,

   In ages to come, shall awake at thy name,

And fond recollections of thee shall be stealing

   Thro' hearts thou hast warm'd with thy heaven-born flame.

Oh ! what are the names that are with'ring before thee ?
　　They will be but as meteors that blaze and expire ; —
But mild shall the glory be fame shall spread o'er thee,
　　And hallow'd for ever the tones of thy lyre.

Thou art like the fair rose that hath drank the sweet shower,
　　And, revived and refresh'd by its dews and its rain,
In incense and soft grateful fragrance, the flower
　　Breathes back the rich treasure to heaven again.

It is said, that the eagle, thro' summer skies flying,
　　Ever fixes his gaze on the bright orb of day,
And they say, that when wounded, and even when dying,
　　He turns to the glory that lighted his way.

And so 'tis with thee, — for thy path hath been glorious;
　　Thou hast look'd up to heav'n for support as thou trod :
And that view — in thy death o'er the tyrant victorious —
　　Shall lift up thy soul to thy Father and God.

STANZAS.

Hast thou not seen when winter hath bound
   In icy chains the river ;
When not a flower adorn'd the ground,
   And nature seem'd sleeping for ever ;
When the earth had thrown off her robe of green ? —
Hast thou not gazed on such a scene ?

Hast thou not sometimes found a bud,
   When that dark season prevaded,
That over the snow that lay round it stood,
   Tho' every other was faded ? —
And did'st thou not prize it, in that dark hour,
More than if blown in a summer bow'r ?

Hast thou not known an hour of woe,

   When sorrow of peace had bereft thee;

When thy heart to the world was as cold as the snow,

   And not one blessing seem'd left thee? —

Hath not a hope sprung up in thy mind

That still could bloom thro' the tempest unkind?

Yes; — that heav'nly hope will still cling

   Round the heart, and will never forsake it,

Prized far more than in life's young spring;

   And tho' sorrow should well nigh break it,

Still would Hope's flower unblasted be placed —

A blossoming bud in a desolate waste.

Hast thou not, on a winter's night,

   Oft on the stars been gazing?

Have they not seem'd to shed fairer light,

   As if their orbs brighter were blazing? —

And hast thou not forgot, in their glow,

The stormy world that lay below?

Is it not thus with the broken heart,

    That from earthly joy is riven?

Do not the thoughts of the world depart,

    When that heart is fix'd on heaven? —

Yes ;— when the soul lies in sorrow and night,

Then is the prospect of heav'n most bright.

YESTERDAY.

And thou I lov'd art gone
   Far over the dark sea ;
That heart is left alone
   That only throbb'd for thee. —
The morning sun is bright,
   The flowers around are gay ; —
But where is the soft light
   Thou shed'st on Yesterday ?

We stood amid these bowers,

    When last I said adieu,

Surrounded by fair flowers

    Of many a brilliant hue.

I kiss'd away the tear

    That dimm'd thine eye's bright ray ; —

But thou no more art near,

    And past is Yesterday.

The summer sun had set

    Deep in the murm'ring sea ;

But his beams linger'd yet —

    They loved to look on thee.

The Zephyrs kiss'd thy lip,

    As if they wooed thy stay ;

And on those waves a ship

    Rode gaily Yesterday.

But thou and that tall bark
 Alike are pass'd and gone ; —
Over the waters dark
 Ye both are sailing on.
Yes ; — thou art gone afar :
 My dream is pass'd away ;
For hidden is the star
 That smiled on Yesterday.

" I SPEAK NOT OF BEAUTY."

" What is the blooming tincture of the skin,
  To peace of mind and harmony within ?"

I speak not of beauty ; — it is not a face

  That can win the affection of hearts such as mine :

I never the sweetness, some fancy, could trace

  In features so cold and insensate as thine.

Thy cheek may be spread with a soft rosy glow ; —

  But it blooms for thine own selfish pleasures alone :

Thy heart may be pure ; — but then 'tis as the snow

  That chills the kind hand that would make it its own.

Thine eye may be bright; — but it hath not the art
   That can throw a soft spell o'er the soul it enslaves —
That can cast its bright fetters around the young heart,
   As the sun-beams are thrown o'er the swift-flowing waves.

And round thy soft lip may lurk many a wile,
   And thy cheek with its blushes all bright may appear; —
But to me there 's no charm in the cold frozen smile,
   That at sympathy's call cannot melt to a tear.

Thy diamonds may shine in thy dark flowing hair,
   And thy gems mock the lustre that beams in thine eye,
And those tresses may wave o'er that bosom so fair,
   That hath never yet heav'd with one pitying sigh.

Oh! give me the jewel that falls from the eye,
   That weeps for the grief of another alone; —
Oh! give me the cheek that can smile itself dry,
   As soon as those sorrows and woes are its own.

Oh ! give me a breast that is fair as the snows,

  Yet warm as the sun-beam that melts them again;

And while it possesses the sweets of the rose,

  As pure as the dew on its leaves may remain.   .

Oh ! give me the maid with a heart that can feel,

  Whose soul with the chain of affection is twin'd,

And a brow on which pity hath set her soft seal ; —

  Oh ! give me the maid with a sensitive mind.

OCEAN:

GRATEFULLY INSCRIBED TO MR. LINFITT OF BURNHAM
ACADEMY.

If ever to mortals sensations are given,
As pledges of purer ones hoped for in heav'n ;
They are those which arise, when, with humble devotion,
We gaze upon thee, thou magnificent Ocean !

BERNARD BARTON.

Oh ! how I love to stand on some high rock,

And gaze upon the foaming wild abyss

Of Ocean — all unshaken by the shock

Of billows beating 'gainst the precipice ! —

To gaze upon the whirl, and hear the hiss

Of thousand surges bursting at its base ! —

To me there is a horrid charm in this —

A charm to see the white foam run its race,

And, as one wave dissolves, another take its place.

Unbounded Ocean ! many a ship o'er thee
Hath swept, — and many another still shall sweep :
Yet of their track no traces can we see ;
Still wildly o'er thy breast the billows leap —
Still over thee, unfathomable deep !
The surges lift their foaming crests in scorn ; —
Still over thee, the winds their revels keep ;
And, as the gallant bark along is borne,
Thou closest o'er its way untrodden and untorn.

I oft have seen thee when the deep red West
Was mirror'd in thee, — and a glossy lake,
Calm and unruffled, seem'd thy peaceful breast,
And not an angry billow was awake, —
When not a breath of air was felt to shake
Thy quiet surface, — and the view on shore
Seem'd of thy gentle beauty to partake, —
While the serene blue sky smiled sweetly o'er,
And the whole scene around a heavenly aspect wore.

And I have gazed upon thee when thy waves
Rose up tumultously, to try their might
With winds and storms, — when billows left their caves
To swell the noises of that dreadful fight; —
E'en 'midst the horrors of a stormy night,
When surges roar'd, and the winds wildly blew,
I have gazed on thee with a stern delight,
And felt as if a part of thee, — and drew
More pleasure from thee as the tempest louder grew.

And I have seen thy billows madly foam,
And chase upon thy breast in hideous throng,
As if they left for ever their deep home,
Thy sunken rocks and hidden caves among;
While, as the wind wax'd stronger and more strong,
The roaring surges, like wild horses, rose
To whirl the chariot of the storm along, —
To deal around them shipwreck, death, and woes,
And rise to Heaven itself, as if its deadliest foes.

By Man the earthly wild may be reclaim'd : —
Unmeasur'd Ocean ! who can rule o'er thee ?
Thy waves still roll — untameable — untam'd :
None can control thee ; — thou art wild and free :
No earthly power can calm thee ; — thou must be
Kept in subjection but by One alone: —
HE, who once calm'd the raging of the sea,
And still to thee, proud Ocean ! will be known ; —
HE holds thee in HIS hand, — thy might is all HIS own.

Thou hast thy creatures too, — a populous world
Of uncouth beings — monsters of the Deep,
That are born there and die : thy billows curl'd,
Mount over caverns where the white pearls sleep ;
And, hid within thy depths, the sea-weeds creep,
And grow beneath the surf that wildly raves,
Unmindful of the storms that o'er them leap,
And the rude winds that lash the dreadful waves,
Until, like beaten hounds, they howling seek thy caves.

Above thee glides the happy mariner, —

All health and life ; — beneath thee is his tomb :

He rides upon thy waters' angry stir,

And little thinks of what shall be his doom : —

He knows not of the dreadful death to come ;

Nor thinks, perchance, the next returning wave

Shall sweep him from the deck and bear him home

To the recesses of some coral cave,

That serves at once for winding-sheet, and hearse, and grave.

GOD is in every thing ; — HIS voice is heard

In the light murmur of the water-fall —

In the gay music of each singing bird,

That tells there is a Providence o'er all ;

But most from thee, oh Ocean ! does HE call,

And in thy wonders admiration claim ; —

And where 'twixt nations stands thy liquid wall,

HE builds the lasting altar of his fame,

And writes on thee in waves HIS Everlasting Name.

Farewell, vast Ocean !— beautiful art thou

In calm and tempest : — now Calm reigns o'er thee ;

Serene and quiet is thy glossy brow,

Thou glorious mirror of the Deity !

And how sublimely grand art thou, when HE,

In foaming characters, upon thy face

Writes HIS almighty anger ! Thou, proud Sea !

Art the wide page — the chosen tablet-place —

On which HE chooses HIS tremendous wrath to trace.

Oh Ocean ! it is o'er thy trackless way,

HE shews himself most mighty : — there HE wields

The sceptre that the winds and waves obey : —

HE rides in storms above thy watry fields.

Thou seemest most HIS own ; — to Man HE yields

Part of the rule o'er earth, — but over thee

HE shows HIS anger, — and HIS mercy shields

The seaman over many a stormy sea, —

And there sweeps many a one into Eternity.

Farewell, vast Ocean!—thou hast borne me home:—

Now, not a wave disturbs thy quiet breast;

But o'er that breast I never more shall roam,

For now my weary wanderings shall find rest;

I go to meet the beings I love best —

Beings from whom I've long been torn apart.

Yes;—I again shall see them and be blest;

And they shall heal the wounds of this worn heart:

I ne'er shall tempt thee more — tho' beautiful thou art.

Farewell!—perchance full many a year will pass,

Before I shall look on thy face again:—

Say, wilt thou be the clear pellucid glass

That now I leave thee?—wilt thou be so then?—

Or wilt thou, in thine anger and disdain,

Throw thy white foam upon this very spot,—

While o'er thee tempests shall assert their reign?

Thou art all silent—and thou answerest not.

Farewell, wide Sea!—this eve will long be unforgot.

1 am not young;—my life has pass'd its prime.

Perhaps I ne'er again shall tread this shore.

Life is a billow on the sea of time

That, once burst, foams and rises never more :—

Perchance mine soon may melt amid the roar

Of tempests rising on that boundless sea ;

Then will my grief and sorrow all give o'er ;—

Then shall *Life's* joy or misery cease to be,

And I shall be resolv'd in vast Eternity.

TO MY GRANDMOTHER,

ON COMPLETING HER EIGHTIETH YEAR.

And thou art grown old, and thy beauty is fled,
   And the hey-day of life and enjoyment is o'er:
On thy once nut-brown locks Time his snow-show'r hath shed,
   And thine eyes are grown dim, and thou now art fourscore.

Yet think not we love thee the less, for the set
   Of the sun of thy beauty, that once shone so fair;
That orb is below the horizon, — and yet
   Its beams shed a lustre and brilliancy there.

The morning may shine all unclouded and bright,

And the sun in his glory all fair may arise ;

But it has not the glow that the farewell of light

Can shed on the breast of the evening skies.

And so, tho' the gay face of beauty is flown,

And the joys of thy youth are all faded away ;

The remembrance of kind acts is over thee thrown,

And angels shall hail thee to mansions of day.

" THE LAST TIME I STOOD BY THIS RIVER."

————

The bird that wanders all day long,
  At sunset seeks her nest : —
I've wandered long.   My native home !
  Now take me to thy rest.

                                    C.

————

The last time I stood by this river,

  The sun was just sinking to rest ;

I parted — and parted for ever,—

  From the maiden I clasp'd to my breast.

Fair flowers around us were blowing,

  That long since have faded away;

And a beam on the cottage was glowing

  That has sunk in the arms of decay.

That elm, that now rises in glory,

   Was then but a sapling plant ;

That shepherd, whose head is grown hoary,

   A youth in industry and want.

The face of the earth seems remoulded,

   Since I last saw my own native clime ;

And full many a change is yet folded

   Within the broad bosom of Time.

But there is one object unalter'd —

   The sun with his heaven-lit flame ; —

The last time I o'er the hill falter'd

   'Twas blazing and burning the same.

It hath gazed on full many a nation,

   When scatter'd in sorrow and woe ; —

It hath look'd o'er the gloom of creation,

   And smiled on our sufferings below.

It hath riṣen in the morn in its brightness, —

    It hath blazed thro' its heav'nly course still, —

It hath sunk in the eve in its brightness,

    Behind the dark shade of that hill.

So 'tis with the good the world's given, —

    Its brightest of dreams will decay;

But the hope that is fixed in heaven

    Can never be faded away.

'T will rise in the blaze of its splendour —

    'T will roll thro' its luminous course; —

In grief, cheering comfort 't will render —

    Thy lasting and brilliant resource.

No gloom from thy heart can divide it —

    Still lit by its soul-cheering ray;

It will sink but when thou sink'st beside it,

    As the sun only sets with the day.

O'er the clouds of thy sorrow 'twill lighten,

    Illuming the shadow beneath ;

And thy evening hour 't will brighten,

    Shining e'en in the Valley of Death.

"I SAW THEE IN LIGHT."

I saw thee in light and in loveliness shining —

Thy beauty all glorious — thy features all fair;

And the modest white pearl with the rose-bud was twining,

Around the bright curls of thy rich auburn hair.

I saw those fair locks on the summer breeze streaming,—

I heard thy soft voice— sweet — and gentle — and low,

And saw thy bright eyes 'neath thy fair forehead beaming,

Two violet buds in their mansion of snow.

I saw those blue eyes dimm'd with sorrow and weeping,

And the smiles that once beam'd there in beauty effaced,

And thy bosom, where joy had been tranquilly sleeping,

The fingers of woe with her sad name had traced.

And I saw thee when all thy dark troubles were ended,

And thou had'st surrender'd thy innocent breath,

And thy pure, happy soul to thy God was ascended,

And thy beautiful features were smiling in death.

FRIENDSHÍP.

Friendship is that pure hallow'd light
  That warms — but burns not with its rays ;
It is not passion's maddening flight —
  It is not frenzy's frantic blaze.

It is the day-beam of the soul —
  The calm content within the breast —
Each angry passion to control,
  And lull each anxious care to rest.

As flies the magnet to the pole —
  The same in darkness clouds and dearth,
So turns congenial soul to soul,
  And Friendship's sunny light hath birth.

And when our course is nearly done,

And all our earthly trials past,

We turn to Friendship's setting sun,

And see it smiling to the last.

ENNISFALL.

When true hearts lie wither'd,
  And fond ones are flown ;
Oh ! who would inhabit
  This bleak world alone ?
                              MOORE.

When last I took a sad farewell

  Of thee — my native Ennisfall,

The cold pale moon-light softly fell

  On the grey turrets of thy hall.

Faded away were those sweet flowers

  That once around thee used to blow,

And on thy wither'd leafless bowers

  There hung pure wreaths of Winter's snow.

But tho' without thee all was dead,

 There were warm hearts within thee then, —

Hearts that around blest influence shed —

 Forms I must never see again.

And it was hard from them to part,

 To wander on a foreign shore —

To leave those dearest to my heart,

 Perhaps to meet them never more '

But tho' I wander'd forth alone,

 And though thou wert no longer fair,

Bright hopes around my heart were thrown

 That sweetly bloom'd and flourish'd there.

It was before Affliction's storm

 Had quench'd in tears their living light,

When Youth's affections all were warm,

 And Life appear'd all fair — all bright.

'Twas then I left thee, Ennisfall,

   While rainbow Hope before me shone ; —

I am return'd at last — and all

   The friends I lov'd are past and gone.

'Twas on a clear cold winter's night,

   I wept for thee my parting tear ; —

The summer round thee now is bright,

   And yet thou art not half so dear.

For they are gone whose lov'd smile threw

   A beauty o'er the darkest scene, —

And I am left alone to view,

   With vacant eye, thy bowers of green.

Thy flowers — thy leaves are nought to me ;

   Thy wreath is dead around my heart ; —

I little care for thine and thee,

   However fair and bright thou art.

Thy flow'rets, by the winter chill'd,

    Bloom'd when fair Spring resum'd her reign; —

My hope, by disappointment kill'd,

    Can never bud and smile again.

STANZAS,

ON THE DEATH OF A YOUNG LADY.

And can it be true, that thy pure happy spirit

    Hath fled from these regions of darkness and death,

In the beautiful mansions of light to inherit

    The glorious palm and the amaranth wreath?

Oh! where are the roses — the lilies — the graces —

    That to every beholder could passion impart? —

Decay and destruction are filling their places,

    And on thy soft bosom hath Death fix'd his dart.

Oh ! where is the hand never backward in bringing

    Relief to the wretch — to the traveller rest ? —

Perhaps round those fingers the earth-worm is clinging,

    And Corruption has fix'd her abode on that breast.

Oh! where are the chords of that heart, whose soft numbers

    Re-echoed to Friendship and Pity alone ? —

The hand of Oblivion is spreading her slumbers

    O'er their liveliest note, and their loveliest tone.

The oak that upon the bleak mountain is growing,

    The storm in its rudeness the firmer may bind ;

But the primrose beneath in the lowly vale blowing

    Cannot brook the rough blast and the tempest unkind.

So fared it with thee, — for the rest could recover,

    Again in new vigour and health to arise ; —

But the bolt of the Tyrant, in passing them over,

    Marked out thy fair form for its beautiful prize.

Farewell to thy spirit! — 'tis fled to its heaven,

  As flew the fair dove to the cherishing ark :

The storms of the world from its refuge have driven

  The diamond, — 'tis fled — and the casket is dark.

FRIENDSHIP AND LOVE.

Friendship's like the moon,
   All our sorrows lightening ; —
But Love is as the sun,
   Burning while 'tis brightening.

Love will not allow
   Another friend beside us ; —
But Friendship serves to show
   Other stars to guide us.

Friendship's moon-beam fair,
   If Misfortune sear us,
Still is smiling there,
   Calmly resting near us.

But if the slightest cloud

   Should pass before Love's day,

He 'll suddenly enshroud

   And steal himself away.

Love is like a flower,

   Delicate and bright,

But faded in an hour,

   Vanish'd ere the night.

But Friendship, like the tree

   Always green before us,

Tho' not so gay as Love may be,

   Still spreads its shelter o'er us.

SONG.

And can'st thou believe that my passion has perish'd,
   Tho' the torrent that first overwhelm'd me is gone:
No ; — first in this heart thy dear image is cherish'd,
   Tho' the stream of affection run silently on.

As the lamps that enliven the tombs of the dead,
   And all the dark vault with their brilliancy fill,
So love round this heart its blest radiance has shed,
   And my passion burns brightly — tho' hiddenly — still.

THE MOURNER TO NEW-YEAR'S DAY.

One fatal remembrance — one sorrow — that throws
  Its bleak shade alike o'er our joys and our woes,
To which life nothing darker nor brighter can bring,
  For which joy has no balm — and affliction no sting.

MOORE.

Roll on, sad year! — thou canst not bring

  Aught that can bless, or injure me. —

Roll on; — and on thy heavy wing

  Bear either joy or misery.

None can affect my heart :— 'tis sear —

  Its feelings long ago are gone.

It cannot hail thee now, sad year!

  It only asks thee to roll on; —

It only longs to see thee o'er,

As many a one hath roll'd before.

H

If thou canst any feeling cast

   Around that heart — tis rather joy,

To think another year is past

   Of life, that grief will soon destroy; —

To think the year that saw my crime,

   Is past with all its load of pain —

A bubble on the sea of time

   That never can apppear again: —

'Tis gone; and thou, New Year! art come,

Perchance, to bear me to the tomb.

'Twas with a smile I hail'd that year,

   Nor knew how full of woe 'twould be; —

l greet *thy* coming with a tear, —

   Say has thy store a hope for me?

A hope for me! — vain useless thought!

   None shall e'er touch this heart again: —

With that deceitful guide, I sought

   For peace — and all my search was vain.

Sorrow may wound — despair decay —

But blasted hope is worse than they.

'Tis only dark futurity
   That is untinged by grief or sin. —
How little know I what may be
   The store of woe thou hast within!
Scarcely had dawu'd thy earliest day,
   Before it heard the voice of woe; —
Scarce had its morn commenced her sway,
   Ere guilt had sullied o'er its snow.
That sigh that told of grief was mine; —
That guilt—my heart that dared repine.

Perchance thou art the last new year
   This tear-dimm'd eye shall ever see; —
Perhaps another happier sphere,
   Ere thou art flown, my rest may be;
For there is nought in this dark scene
   To tempt my sorrowing soul to stay:
With joy 'twill leap the gulf between
   It and the realms of endless day.
May its repinings be forgiven
And my sad heart find rest in heav'n!

"THEY MAY TALK OF THEIR FLOWERS."

They may talk of their flowers, and the crimson that blushes,
  Thc Queen of the garden, the rose on its tree ; —
But while I'm possess'd of thy innocent blushes,
  I care for none else, — they're the roses for me.

They may talk of their diamond that beams in the mine ;
  It sparkling and glowing and brilliant may be ; —
But while thy dear eyes with benevolence shine,
  I care for none else, — they're the diamonds for me.

They may talk, if they will, of their Venus resplendent
  With beauty and life, as she sprang from the sea ;
They may talk of the cestus, hcr graceful attendant ; —
  But Love is the cestus that binds me to thee.

LAMENT FOR A HIGHLAND CHIEFTAIN.

'Tis he! — Our noble Chieftain lies

Stretch'd on the turf before our eyes;

His life-blood on the heathery ground

Drops slowly from the stiff'ning wound.

  Tho' the hostile army flieth,

    Widely scatter'd o'er the plain,

  Icy cold in death he lieth,

    Mingling with the lowly slain.

  He is gone — our glorious chief —

  Lasting be our tears and grief!

Beside him lies his faithful serf,

Bleeding and lifeless, on the turf, —

He, who still near his master kept,

Watch'd o'er him when fatigued he slept —

   Sought with him, the hottest battle —

     Shielded him he lov'd so well —

   Unappall'd heard cannon rattle —

     Then with his brave Chieftain fell.

Mac Morven did not die alone; —

Mourn them both — they both are gone.

We will not bear them to his hall,

Nor lay them 'neath the funeral pall; —

We will not chant the Coronach, —

It would not call their spirits back.

   Lay them both beneath the heather,

     Each wrapp'd in his bloody plaid ; —

   They will soundly sleep together,

     'Neath that weeping birch tree's shade.

Their rest will be as quiet there,

As 'neath piles of marble fair.

Oh strew no flowers upon the grave:—

There will the purple heather wave;

And summer suns and vernal showers

Refresh its hardy leaves and flowers.

Now the sun's last light diminish'd

Scarcely shows the western hill:—

Now our mournful task is finish'd;

But we linger near them still.

They are sleeping 'neath the turf—

Farewell, brave Chief, and faithful serf!

" FAREWELL, THOU FALSE ONE!"

Then farewell, thou false one !—Ah! who'd have thought Sin
  In that fond seeming heart could have e'er been a guest?
And that Folly and Vice could be rankling within
  The fair snowy bounds of that beautiful breast?

Thy form by thy beauty was all lighted up;
  But within it was sorrow,— beneath it was death :
As the blush that is thrown o'er the winebibber's cup;
  But colours the woe that is lurking beneath.

The heaven, when 'tis seen in the day-time afar,
  May seem faultless in beauty, and shining in light;
But deprived of each beautiful fair-beaming star,
  Oh how dark would it be in the gloom of the night!

And it is as thee ; — for thy beauty may glow

    Without virtue, e'en bright 'neath the blaze of thy heaven ; —

But when Pleasure's gay sun is quick sinking below

    The horizon of life, — oh ! how dark will be even !

Oh ! who would have thought that the soft smiling rays

    Which thy bright-beaming eyes oft upon me would dart,

Could e'er have become the volcano's wild blaze,

    To consume all the hopes of this once happy heart ?

Then farewell, thou false one ! for ever I'm gone ; —

    I leave thee — the sport of thy hopes and thy fears —

To brood o'er thy folly and suffering alone ;

    To heave penitent sighs, and shed penitent tears.

STANZAS.

In vain my lyre would lightly breathe ; —
  The smile that sorrow fain would wear
Mocks but the rose that lurks beneath,
  Like roses o'er a sepulchre.

LORD BYRON.

Nay ;—ask not for a mirthful air,—
  I ne'er will sing of joy again ;
Dejected—driven to despair—
  As I for ever must remain ;

Nor bid me tell of happier days,
  When hope was young, and life look'd sweet ;
When all my light was pleasure's blaze,
  And joys were smiling at my feet.

But let me sing of wounded peace, —

    A mind by passion's conflict torn, —

Of lost content, — of ruin'd ease,

    And hopes that died as soon as born, —

Of fancy's self-destroying dreams, —

    Of disappointment's fatal dart, —

These, and these only, are the themes

    That suit a woe-worn broken heart.

That heart is sick with hope deferr'd ; —

    Its dreams are false — its prospects vain —

And friendship's voice is never heard,

    To calm my wilder'd fev'rish brain.

Despair within my bosom preys ;—

    You *see* not—but I *feel* the smart:

Like Ætna's wild internal blaze,

    It silently consumes my heart.

Sometimes reflection's lurid beam

    Will dart like madness o'er my mind ;

And, as a baleful meteor stream

    To show the dreadful wreck behind.

And sometimes hope's delusive light

    Will, for an instant, o'er me roll,

And with its sunshine-ray make bright

    Even the darkness of *my* soul.

But soon of joy I lose the trace : —

    That beam allow'd me but to see

The cavity — the dreadful space —

    That lies between my peace and me.

Then go; and follow pleasure's course;

    And leave me to my tears and sighs,

And to the torture of remorse

    That ever-dying never dies.

GREECE:

AFFECTIONATELY INSCRIBED TO C. T. ROBERTSON, ESQ.

———

Oh, let grief come first,
O'er pride itself victorious,
To think how man hath curst
What Heaven hath made so glorious !

MOORE,

———

The flowers still bloom in fair Ionia's isles;

On Marathon the summer sun still smiles ;

The zephyr in the balmy evening breathes,

And sighs and whispers o'er fair flow'ry wreaths ;

The nightingale, from waving cypress boughs,

Pours to the blushing rose melodious vows ;—

But yet a something breathes throughout the scene,

That says, more lovely still it once hath been ; —

A something, like the sad dejected air

That hangs around fond beauty in despair.

Oh, Greece ! what is it makes thy present state

So beautiful, — and yet so desolate?

Renders thy sons so servile and so weak,

And steals the rose from every daughter's cheek,

And makes thee — tho' so lovely — only seem

The fading image of some glorious dream ?

Yet why enquire ? I've but to look around,

To see thy sons in foreign fetters bound,

To see those once brave spirits now so tame,

Wounded and broken— Grecian but in name ;—

To see the gath'ring weeds that freely wave

Above the tomb of thy departed brave ;—

To see the ivy that uncultur'd twines

Around thy ruin'd fanes, and mouldering shrines ; —

To look on temples, time had spared, defaced

By ruthless hands, and by the Turk laid waste ;—

These to the question silently reply,

For but one glance thrown o'er them, --" Tyranny !"

And it is so. — Upon thy Marathon,

Where once thy valour nobly, proudly, shone,

Now the insulting Moslem casts his chain,

And thy sons crouch submissive to his reign.

And where is Sparta? — Where is Sparta's King? —

Low in the dust they both are mouldering.

Nought but her ruins stand, — and the wild grass

Grows o'er the grave of her Leonidas.

And Athens too, where fair Minerva reign'd —

Where eloquent Demosthenes enchain'd

The list'ning ear, — where glorious Phocion spoke ; —

Is she too sunk beneath the oppressor's yoke?

No — not quite fall'n : but ah, how sadly changed !

By Moslem feet her marble pavement ranged : —

Her heroes and her orators are gone ;

And there insensibly she moulders on.

Departed days of grandeur and of bliss !

Are ye and all your greatness come to this ?

Rise ! rise, ye Grecians ! burst the servile yoke,

And break your fetters, as your fathers broke.

Oh think upon your sires' " Thermopylæ ;—

And make a glorious effort to be free !''

Oh, Grecia ! cease beneath thy foes to weep;—

Thy spirits are not dead — they only sleep ;

And they will rise and wipe away thy tears,

And Liberty will reign thro' future years.

Yes !—they will rouse themselves, and every nerve

Be strain'd to crush the tyrants that they serve ;

And thou shalt break, at length thy galling chain,

Shake off those tyrants,—and be Greece again !

" TO-MORROW, DEAR DEPARTED ONE !"

Oh ! what are thousand living loves
To that which cannot quit the dead ?

LORD BYRON.

To-morrow, dear departed one !

I 'll seek thy lonely grave,

Where the meek primrose opes its buds,

And weeping willows wave.

It was a bright and blushing morn,

My dearest, when you died : —

That summer-day that dawn'd so fair,

I was to be thy bride.

I wove myself a bridal wreath
   Of flowers of brightest bloom : —
I wore them not, — for they were laid
   To wither on thy tomb.

Were they not emblems of the hopes
   That once so sweetly bloom'd
Around my heart?   But now they're gone, —
   With thee they're all entomb'd.

To-morrow evening, then, lost Love !
   When the last sun-beam sets,
I'll weave that grave an April wreath —
   A wreath of violets.

I planted there two fair rose trees :
   One sunk in quick decay;
But leaf by leaf, and flower by flower,
   The other drops away.

Then I will love that lonely tomb,

And that slow-fading tree —

The emblems of my wither'd hope,

My blighted love and me.

VERSES

WRITTEN AFTER READING THE ANACREONTIC SONG IN " THE LIGHT OF THE HARAM," IN MOORE'S " LALLAH ROOKH."

Domestic Happiness! thou only bliss
Of Paradise that hath survived the fall!

COWPER.

It is not in the hall where the sparkling wine flows,

   That pleasure, and peace, and contentment are found ; —

For me there is far more enjoyment in those

   Dear faces, that now I see smiling around.

It is not in the visions of Folly and Mirth,

   That the purest of joy and of happiness is ; —

But oh ! " if there be an Elysium on earth,

     It is this, it is this !"

Yes ; — 'tis pleasure indeed to behold each fond face,

    That in health and contentment are smiling here now :

To gaze on each being I love so — and trace

    A calm satisfaction on each happy brow ;

To feel the fond love that with life had its birth,

    And to know it unalter'd — 'tis exquisite bliss !

" And oh ! if there be an Elysium on earth,

        It is this, it is this !"

Oh ! who ever would sing of the charms of the bowl,

    Or spend on its praises one strain or one word,

Who had felt the dear magical ties of the soul,

    And domestic delight that awaken'd each chord ?

To sit on an evening like this, round the hearth,

    And to feel the soft touch of a sisterly kiss —

If there ever could " be an Elysium on earth,

        It is this, it is this !"

Oh! I wish not a deeper delight than is known

    To my heart in such gentle enjoyments as these :

Tho' the storms have past o'er us, no blossom hath blown,

    From the light sapling plant, or the deep-rooted trees ;

By their smiles all the love of my heart is call'd forth,

    As the sun draws the scent from the rose by its kiss ; —

" And oh ! if there be an Elysium on earth,

        It is this, it is this."

THE MANIAC.

I know, my love, thou art false to me;
  Yet I cannot love thee less:
And I know I have lost the little power
  I once might have to bless.

I know to-morrow will see thee wed
  To a young and beautiful bride; —
And I know thou wilt think no more of me,
  Who was once thy joy and thy pride.

I am near the grave with grief and despair;
  And the merry marriage bell
That summons thy bride and thee to church,
  Will be my funeral knell.

Thy bride is young — thy bride is fair —

   May her virtues long fix thee !

And oh ! may'st thou never be false to her,

   As thou hast been to me !

Yet think not, love, that at my death,

   My spirit from thee will part ; —

I still will guard and watch over thee,

   Tho' thou hast broken my heart.

When thou and thy fair bride shall gaze

   On the rosy evening sky —

When the sun hath set in the western sea —

   Invisibly I will be nigh.

And when summer smiles, I will appear

   Like a fair and beautiful rose ;

And thou, perchance, wilt admire me,

   And say my blush brightly glows.

I-will weep a drop of purest dew,

    And breathe the most fragrant sigh

That ever flower on earth yet breathed,

    When thou and thy bride come nigh.

I will whisper amidst the breezes of eve ; —

    I will swell the nightingale's song ;

And my breath shall perfume the fair young flowers

    And groves thou walkest among.

I will watch o'er thee when thou sleepest, love,—

    I will float on the soft moon-beams —

To whisper music in thine ear,

    And lull thee with heavenly dreams.

And when at last thou shalt die, my love,

    A primrose I'll over thee bloom ;

And my soul shall dissolve in a dew-drop tear,

    For a willow to weep o'er thy tomb.

SHE DREAMETH.

—— There it lies — so tranquil — so beloved, —
   All that it hath of Life with us is living ;
So gentle, stirless, helpless, and unmoved,
   And all unconscious of the joy 'tis giving.

Lord Byron.

She sleeps within a blooming bower,

And around her is many a summer flower,

And the fragrant winds that wander there

Stir the wavy curls of her auburn hair,

That is wreath'd with flowers of jessamine meek : —

There 's a smile on her lip, and a blush on her cheek ;

   And of something sweet she dreameth.

Is she dreaming now of her native home,

And the spots where in childhood she loved to roam?

Is she calling back the sportive hours

When she wove her garlands of fresh wild flowers,

When her soul dwelt as free in its own sweet world,

As the wind that waves her ringlets curl'd?

    No;—not of these she dreameth.

Or does she dream of that blessed shore

Where grief and tears shall be no more,

Where nought can go but what hath shown

A spirit as guileless and pure as her own,

Where never was known a sorrow or crime,

And Joy feels not the bonds of time?

    Not of this—not of this she dreameth.

Is her spirit now, with a dreamer's scope,

Passing o'er the sunny bowers of Hope,

And winging its way, with an eagle's flight,

Thro' her skies that smile in unclouded light,

Far away from the scenes of mortal strife,

And forgetting awhile the shackles of life ?

  Not of these — not of these she dreameth.

Doth she now with Fancy's eye recall

When she bid farewell to her father's hall, —

When she blushing left her mother's side,

And with smiles and tears became my bride ?

Is she dreaming o'er the time when she

Consented to leave them all for me ?

  Perhaps of this she dreameth.

Hark ! she murmurs something in her sleep —

And the blush on her cheek becomes more deep —

And a gentle sigh from her bosom heaves,

Soft as wind that stirs the aspen leaves ; —

Again that sigh breathes out the same ; —

And oh ! she softly whispers *my* name —

    'Tis of me ! 'tis of me she dreameth !

DISAPPOINTMENT.

The Hope that once blest us is faded and dead;
 Our prospects are vanish'd, our transports are o'er;
The ray that hath lighted our pathway is fled,
 And the vision that cheer'd us can cheer us no more.

Like flowers that lay sleeping in safety below
 The earth's frozen surface, while icy blasts chill'd,
Too prompt at the first April sun-beam to blow,
 Till Winter return'd — and the blossoms were kili'd:

So perish'd our Hopes; for they flourish'd awhile
 Beneath the warm ray that had first lured them on;
Till, tempted too far by its dangerous smile,
 The winter-wind blew, — and the sun-beam was gone.

The rose tree will spread its fair flowers to the morn,

   Till the night-blast hath crush'd it too rudely to earth ;

'Twill fall — and, in falling, a merciless thorn

   'Twill plant in the bosom on which it had birth.

So it is with our Hopes ; — they 're too brilliantly blown,

   To resist the rude breath of Misfortune unkind ;

But the roses all wither'd — the blossoms all strown, —

   They will leave their sharp thorns with their parent the mind.

But tho' Disappointment we cannot withstand ;

   And tho' the rude tempest we cannot defy,

Yet there is a bountiful merciful hand

   That will wipe all the tears from the sorrowing eye.

Tho' our flowers are wither'd, and scatter'd our fruit,

   And tho' earthly comfort far from us be driven,

A fair branch shall spring from our mouldering root,

   And bear flowers that cannot be wither'd in heaven.

THE RECLUSE TO THE WORLD.

World ! I have bid thee long farewell,
   And never wish to taste again
The joys and cares that in thee dwell.
   The cup of pleasure or of pain
Is nought to me ; — no Sorrows reign
   To shadow o'er my quiet cell.
None of thy hopes delude my brain,
   That I might hear their early knell
Ring in mine ears.   No ; — I have given
My thoughts — hopes — feelings — all, to heaven.

Yet in this holy solitude —

   Although so separate from thee —

Remembrance sometimes will intrude

   Of things that once were dear to me;

And though I strongly strive to think

   Of higher things, — 'tis all in vain;

For still with thee there is a link

   That, often burst, still forms again : —

Then, e'en within these holy walls,

The tear of human feeling falls.

And sometimes when the anthem rolls,

   Re-echoed by the convent dome,

While others lift above their souls,

   My thoughts will turn to happy home ;

And when my soul, pour'd out in prayer,

   Should like the incense rise above,

My heart — my feelings all are there,

   And dreaming o'er my early love ; —

But oh ! such feelings should not be ;

For earthly thoughts are not for me.

But hark ! the solemn vesper bell

   Proclaims the hour of prayer is near ;

And I must haste my beads to tell,

   Nor dare to linger longer here.

I will not think — it must not be —

   Down — down, my heart! forget to swell ! —

Vain earth ! I will not think of thee.

   World, and ye worldly cares, — farewell !

Sighs, breathe not ! — tears, forbear to start ' —

Mine shall not be a human heart.

STANZAS.

There is something sadly sweet in the sigh
    That we heave at a transient parting ;—
There is something of loveliness then in the eye
    That smiles thro' its tears is darting—
A strange sweet mixture of pleasure and pain,
When we part, yet are certain of meeting again.

Those sighs of early fondness speak —
    The hope of meeting to-morrow, —
That tear that steals down the rosy cheek
    Is the dew of affection — not sorrow —
Ere the chords of the heart are wrench'd and wrung
From those round whom they have fondly clung.

But oh ! it is sad to part from all
   The earthly ties that bind us,
And know not if ever again we shall
   Meet the beings we leave behind us :
Or, if we should *meet* them, find them estranged,
Tho' our own affections may still be unchanged.

If friendless be the human mind,
   But weak and sad are its powers :
Souls must be like the summer wind
   That wanders o'er smiling flowers,
Kisses the blossom and sighs round the stem,
And only receives its sweetness from them.

Tho' brightly shine the stars above,
   Yet one is brightest and nearest ; —
So, tho' many friends we love,
   One will still be the dearest ;
And, when we wander away afar,
Tho' all shine — but one is our polar star.

That must be the´tie Affliction first form'd,

 That never yet hath forsaken

The being to whom the young heart first warm'd, —

 Whose faith hath never been shaken ; —

One who in pleasure, and sorrow too,

We oft have proved, and still found true.

One who, when perchance we have err'd

 In the days of youthful fólly,

Hath call'd us back, like a wandering bird,

 To the ways of the just and holy ; —

Pointed the path that saints have trod —

Show'd the way, and led us to God.

One on whom we can rely —

 A bond of Virtue's own sealing ;

This is Friendship's firmest tie, —

 This is her purest feeling :

It is Affection's loveliness —

It is Love in his holiest dress. .

THE IVY IN WINTER.

I love to see the ivy wind
　　Its peaceful way around the tree ; —
I love to see its chaplet twined
　　When all around is winterly.

When summer flowers have ceased to bloom —
　　When other leaves around are strown —
When the earth seems a mighty tomb,
　　That ivy flourishes alone.

When Nature's face hath lost its charms —
　　When summer sun-beams cease to bless,
It climbs that tree's rude leafless arms,
　　Subduing it by gentleness.

When clouds and storms no longer reign,

   And Winter droops his sullen wing,

How brightly will it shine again

   Amid'st the gayest flowers of Spring.

And so it is with spirits mild ; —

   They combat danger and distress —

They journey thro' life's devious wild,

   Subduing all by gentleness.

They calmly through its deserts stray,

   Tho' oft by thorns and cares perplex'd ; —

They smile upon the world's decay,

   Weaving a chaplet for the next.

"I SAW IN THE EVENING."

I saw in the evening a soft-flowing stream ;
    Its waves were all sleeping — its ripple at rest—
And the mellowing light of the moon's amber beam
    Was tranquilly bright'ning that rivulet's breast.

I saw when fair Luna gave place to the dawn,
    And the stars one by one dropp'd away to repose,
And the mists of the morning were yet unwithdrawn
    From the sun, where they curtain'd his chamber of rose.

I gazed on the stream ;— it was quiet and still —
    And all noiseless and dark it roll'd silently on—
'Till the sun rais'd his head from the far eastern hill,
    And looked on that stream, and its quiet was gone.

And at noon o'er the brook, its fierce ray the orb roll'd,
 And tho' in its efforts to warm it, it fail'd,
(For e'en in the blaze of mid-day it was cold),
 The rill's crystal breast by the heat was exhaled.

I look'd on the stream,—and I thought of the mind
 That calmly was sleeping in comfort and ease,
When the light of contentment to gloom was consign'd ;
 Oh ! where would it turn for a moment of peace ?

Amidst dissipation, ' twould plunge the lost soul ;
 In the light of false pleasure and folly ' twould sink :
'Twould fly for relief to the poisonous bowl,
 And large draughts of bitterness madly would drink.

And the lightning of vice o'er the erring would dart,
 And the fierce sun of pleasure its madd'ning ray ;
And, tho' it might oft fail to warm the cold heart,
 Like the sun o'er the waters, 'twould waste it away.

THE VALLEY OF ROSES.

———

There the Rose, o'er crag and vale,
Sultana of the nightingale,
   The maid for whom his melody,
   His thousand songs, are heard on high,
Blooms blushing to her Lover's tale.

Lord Byron.

THE VALLEY OF ROSES.

Would you know where young Love in his beauty reposes,
  And find him uninjured by sorrow or care, —
Go — seek for the boy in the Valley of Roses,
  And find the pure Spirit of Constancy there.
'Tis such a sweet Valley ! — Its roses in blowing
  Breathe out a perfume that no other can match,
And the light summer breezes but leave them more glowing,
  And blushing the deeper for kisses they snatch.
They say, that wherever young Passion reposes,
  Tho' the spot be a desert his light makes it fair ; —

And, when he smiles over the Valley of Roses,

    Oh ! what an Elysium of beauty is there !

The sighs of delight that the Lover is breathing

    Mix sweet with the scents from the jessamine bough ; —

And ah ! fair are thy garlands that maidens are wreathing,

    When destin'd to blush on some brides happy brow ;

On the flowers of that Valley when moonlight reposes,

    It shows the bright dew-drops that rest there at even : —

They are Angels' tears wept o'er the Valley of Roses,

    To think e'en that spot is less lovely than Heaven.

    The sun hath risen upon the vale ;

    No longer sings the Nightingale ;

    The night-dew leaves the fresh-blown roses,

      Kiss'd by the sun to heaven again ;

    And every flower and bud uncloses

      Its leaves to blush and brighten then.

    Pass'd off is Night, who, dewy finger'd,

      Shut up the flowers and wet the stem ;

    Chased by the Morn as late she linger'd,

      To take a parting look at them ;

And butterflies are round them flying,

   Waving in light their glittering wings,

That seem as if they had been dying

   In those celestial-tinctur'd springs,

Where new made Seraphs dip their plumes

Ere bathing them in Heaven's perfumes.

   Oh ! what a heaven that Valley seems !

Fair as the fondest dreamer dreams ;

Lovely as Aden,* ere the fall

Of sinful man had blasted all.

Oh ! if there be a spot below

Unstain'd by crime — untinged by woe —

A little spot that scaped the worst,

When all the other world was curst —

A place for Alla's † angels kept

To wave their wings o'er while they wept

The fall of man — a footstool given

To rest them on twixt earth and heaven —

      * Eden.   † God.

If such a place this world discloses,
That spot must be the Vale of Roses.

But there was one who wander'd there
To whom that Valley was not fair,
One, who from earliest youth had been
Familiar with the lovely scene,
Who once delighted walk'd those bowers,
And stopped sometimes to pluck the flowers,
Or chased the large blue butterfly, *
That like a sapphire stream went by,
And laugh'd to see the breezes shake
Her image in the silver lake,
And seem to stir her mirror'd hair,
While she unmoved was standing there; —
But now she doth not stop to look
On flowers — or watch the quivering brook ;
And the bright sky-tinged butterflies,
May pass unheeded by her eyes.

* The large blue butterfly of Cashmere.

Touch'd by some sorrow she appears,

For oh! those eyes are full of tears,

Her former griefs have pass'd away,

Like clouds before a summer day

That flew across a smiling sky,

But marr'd not its serenity;

Yet still the form of clouds to keep,

Oft threaten'd, yet forbore to weep.

But there was something darker now

In Zela's eye—on Zela's brow,

Something that sadly told of more

Grief, than she e'er had felt before.

There is another wandering there

Who shares in Zela's every care,

With her he oft had sought these bowers,

For her had wreath'd their rosy flowers,

With her thro' fairest scenes had roved,

With her had smiled—with her had loved:

But duty call'd him from that blessed shore,

And they must part—perhaps to meet no more.

The lovers met;—oh, who can tell

Those scenes where lovers say farewell !

The quivering lips that will not speak,

Lest with the words a sigh should break,

And tears should overflow the eye,

The pledges of how true the sigh,

Those eyes that keep their steady gaze

Fix'd on each other's mournful face,

Until the heart can bear no more,

And ah ! relievingly, flows o'er.

The tears that flow'd from either lover,

   Although they were suppress'd at first,—

Like thunder-clouds that long may hover,

   But must at last from fullness burst. —

At length the power of speech awoke ;

And Hassan to his Zela spoke,

And in a Lover's tenderest tone,

Sooth'd Zela's woes, and half forgot his own.

" Nay Zela, dearest ! weep not so !

" Tho' Hassan far away must go,

" Thro' a far distant land to range,

" Oh Zela! he will never change.

" I will not wander love for long,

" Our army and our power is strong,

" Duty fulfill'd, I'll cease to roam,

" And thou wilt hail thy wand'rer home.

" Then here thro' life I will remain,

" And never leave my love again.

" 'Till then let Hope's fair light illume

" Thy cheek and wake again its bloom;

" Come, love, the morning wears away,

" I must not here much longer stay;

" Come, go with Hassan up the dell,

" Then kiss him once, and say farewell!"

She could not answer save by look,

But silently his arm she took,

And nothing conscious how she went,

But that on Hassan's arm she leant,

Who, tho' deep his own bosom's wound,

Talk'd of the flowers and birds around,

And tried to smile, to chase a part

Of those thick clouds around her heart.

" Look dearest ! where that Huma * flies,

" A living rainbow thro' the skies,

" My journey surely well will speed,

" It waves its pinions o'er my head !

" Zela ! rememb'rest thou that maids

" Say, whosoe'er the Huma shades

" Need never fear Misfortune's frown,

" For one day he will wear a crown ?"

It was indeed a Huma's wing

That o'er his head was shadowing,

Just pois'd o'er him its plumes of light,

Then darted swiftly out of sight.

Zela looked up and thro' her tears

She smiled, — the hope of happy years

Spent by the side of him she loved,

Had almost half her woe removed,

---

* The Huma is a bird peculiar to the East, where there is a superstition prevalent, that whoever it overshadows will in time wear a crown.

The gloom of parting was forgot,

A flower sprang in that desert spot.

A flower by superstition planted,

   That rose the weeds of woe above;

But tho' by Fancy's power enchanted,

   Its nurses still were Hope and Love.

Yes; — Hope *was* living in her soul

To keep dark sorrow in control;

And when the pair had cross'd the dell —

She almost calmly said, Farewell!

Three years have gone over the Valley of Roses,

   And each shed as it went some new charm from its wing;

More blossoms and beauty that valley discloses,

   As if Nature there loved all her glories to fling.

Tho' old Time in his flight o'er fair Nature oft misses

   To gaze on the beauties he passes the while; —

Oh! he surely would pause o'er that valley of blisses,

   And his features for once would relax to smile.

Oh! there there is something that sweetly disposes

   The saddest to love, by its softness beguiled ;

And could Eblis himself reach the Valley of Roses,

   Tho' demon he is — he had long ago smiled.

Three years that soft Valley of sweets have gone over,

   And every thing there has grown lovelier but one —

'Tis poor Zela, — oft morn dawn'd with Hopes of her lover, —

   Yet evening return'd and still found her alone.

   'Tis evening now, — the sun is setting

     Behind the distant palm-cloth'd hill;

   The dew of night the flowers is wetting ;

     The evening wind just curls the rill ; —

   A weary warrior stops to lave

   His burning brow in that cool wave ; —

   His dress was stain'd and travel-soil'd

   Like one who long and far had toil'd, —

   And the torn weather-beaten vest

   Scarcely conceal'd his sun-burnt breast.

   He stoop'd beside the brook: just then

   Came Zela slowly down the glen, —

Stopp'd — look'd upon the stranger's face ; —

Then scream'd and sank in his embrace :

" Oh dearest love ! 'tis he, 'tis he !

" Hassan returns to comfort me !"

" Yes Zela ! Hassan *is* return'd ;

" But ah ! Hope's fairy light that burn'd

" When last we parted, love, is gone ;

" And I am here — poor — weak — alone ;

" All that I now can bring to thee

   " Is the bright flame that love hath lighted ; —

" All that the fates have left to me

   " Are Love's fair flowrets still unblighted.

" But ah my Zela ! say canst thou

" Love thy poor wandering Hassan now ?"

   " And can'st thou, dearest, doubt my love ?

" Oh ! if there be a Heaven above —

" If the bright star that shineth there

" Still roll its glories thro' the air,

" They both may witness my fond vow, —

   " I never loved thee more than now.

" Hassan ! thou may'st be desolate —

" But let the darkest frown of fate

" Work upon thee its deadliest will, —

" Yet I am Zela — Zela still !

" Doth not the sun as brightly gleam

" On broken wave as quiet stream ; —

" The wind may shake — disturb the rill —

" The sun-light smileth o'er it still ;

" The dew that bathes the blooming bowers

" Spares not to weep o'er wither'd flowers ;

" And thus the Sun of Love may shine

" O'er hearts as sorrow-worn as thine ; —

" And ah ! Affection's tears will fall

" O'er wither'd hopes — reviving all."

" Then Zela I am truly blest !

" How could I doubt thy faithful breast !

" But love, 'twere well we now should part —

" Let it not wound thy gentle heart ;

" I leave thee for a little while —

" Come, bless me with a parting smile :

" To-morrow night the Valley's Lord,

" Of whom thou doubtless oft hast heard,

" The richest one in all the East

" Holds in this vale a splendid feast —

" And here in all the pomp of pride

" Will wed a young and lovely bride;

" And I should like to show him mine

" As lovelily as his can shine.

" Then, when the Muezzin * calls to prayer

" My Zela, I will meet thee there.

" Be at the feast — then farewell, sweet!

" To-morrow night again we meet!"

Ere she could answer he was gone,

And she was standing there alone;

And all the scene was still around —

She heard not e'en his footstep's sound —

So strew'd with blossoms was the ground.

* One who from the mosques proclaims the hour of morning or evening prayer.

She stood — as if 'twere all a dream —

   A dream from which she soon would waken;

For like a vision it must seem

   To be so found — and so forsaken.

   Night fled — the morning quickly pass'd —

Noon blaz'd — and evening came at last!

But oh! no evening ever fell

So lovely on that lovely dell.

The sun set — and the evening star,

Showing its twinkling light afar,

Seem'd the fair signal to give birth

To twice ten thousand stars of earth;

For every rose-bush on that night

Seem'd budding — blossoming in light;

And every tree that vale about

With fiery flow'rets sparkled out,

Hanging on high their starry wreaths, —

While from the trees sweet perfume breathes

From those bright flower-like censors shed,

That with rich Atar-gul * are fed.

       * Otto of Roses.

It seem'd as if a Peri's hand
Had waved o'er all her magic wand,
And bid the gay enchantment rise,
And make a mimic Paradise.

And Zela thro' the joyous throng
Trembling yet quickly glides along,
Until she reaches that gay hall,
Where is the highest festival ;
Then timidly looks round to see
If Hassan with the crowd may be.
A voice—she knew not whence it came—
Just lowly breathed out Zela's name ;
She turns and starts — it cannot be !
But—yes—the voice was his—'tis he !
And now she trembles at his feet.
　She sees in him the Valley's Lord !
" I promised, Zela, we would meet ;
　" And dearest ! I have kept my word.
" Now, Zela, thou art all my own,—
　" Thy place henceforth is by my side.

" Come share with me my princely throne ··

   " My people's Queen!—My lovely bride!

" Remember, love, I prophesied

   " When that bright Huma o'er us flew,

" That I should wear a crown in pride ; —

   " And oh ! my Zela shares it too !"

Farewell to the beautiful Valley of Roses, —

   I leave it and never shall visit it more ;

But I long shall remember the sweets it discloses,

   The fragrance it breath'd, and the flowrets it bore.

May the sunshine long fall on its leaves and its flowers,

   While the butter-flies flutter and sport round each stem ;

May no thunder-cloud ever o'ershadow its bowers,

   Or cast the least tinge of its darkness on them.

Still, still, be it rich in its flowrets and blossoms,

    And sweet be the perfume its roses exhale;

Like the love that lights up fond affectionate bosoms,

    That each moment breathes out, and yet never can fail.

Oh! many a minstrel a sweet song composes

    Of the love that so long and so deeply was tried; —

And sings of the Lord of the Valley of Roses,

    And Zela his faithful, his beautiful bride.

SACRED PIECES.

THE SABBATH.

Hark ! hark !   The Sabbath bells
  Are calling us to prayer :
Their sound floats over hills and dells,
  Borne on the morning air : —
Now swelling with the swelling breeze ;
Now ceasing, as its murmurs cease.

They tell us 'tis the time
  To seek for heavenly love —
To cleanse the heart from guilt and crime,
  And raise the soul above :
They warn us on this holy day
To cast our earthly thoughts away.

It is the day to rest —

To quit our earthly things —

To let each thought within the breast

Rise on Devotion's wings —

To lay our bosoms' secrets bare,

And crush the evil lurking there.

It is the day to weep —

To sorrow for our sin :

The time the strictest watch to keep

On thoughts that work within, —

To humble all ourselves before

Our God, and tremblingly adore.

It is the day of grace —

The day to be forgiven —

The time to seek the Saviour's face,

And fix our hearts on heaven ; —

To bow before his mighty throne,

From whom we hope for grace alone.

It is the time to smile,
    Grateful for mercies past ——
For blessings we receive the while,
    And hope for to the last; ——
To thank the Lord, who thus would bless,[1]
Yet feel our own unworthiness.

It is the time to love——
    To know each tie is dearer ——
To feel the links that nature wove,
    Are to the heart the nearer ;
For what is sweeter on this day,
Than, with the hearts we love, to pray ?

It is the time to hope ——
    To look beyond the tomb ——
To give our spirits wider scope,
    And let them higher roam,
And, with the piercing eye of Faith,
See thro' the shadowy veil of death.

And oft, upon this day,

I've heard the Sabbath bell

Toll forth the mournful sign to lay

One in his narrow cell —

To moulder in his native dust,

Till earth again resign her trust.

Our Sabbaths *here* are short :

Oh ! may we be forgiven ;

And make them the divine support

To lead us up to Heaven !

For blessed souls by praise and prayer

Make an Eternal Sabbath *there*.

TO THE JESSAMINE.

Thou simply blooming — sweetly scenting plant,

   Thou deck'st the humble cotter's lowly door ;

Thou fair companion of distress and want,

   Thou seem'st to love the dwellings of the poor.

Emblem of HIM, who for awhile declining

   The joys the starry courts above could give,

And all HIS regal dignity resigning,

   Dwelt with the humble that our souls might live !

Oh ! what but strong eternal love like this,

   Could quit the Heavenly Angels, who adore

In that bright seat of life — and light — and bliss,

   And be the poorest of the very poor ?

Then, simple blossom, still with flowers o'erspread

   The peasant's cot, and fragrance round it shed.

"I HEARD HER PRAY."

I heard her pray ere passion glow'd
   In crimson blushes on her cheek :
Like Angels' hymns the accents flow'd,
   As pure, as heavenly, and as meek :
With eye and brow all gentleness,
And heart as pure and passionless.

'Twas sweet to see, in life's young hour,
   Ere sorrow's tear had time to start,
Like the first incense from a flower,
   The words rise from that spotless heart.
Yes ; — sweet to hear those soft lips try
A prayer, ere yet they breathed a sigh.

I heard her pray: the happy morn
  Of life was bursting on her sight;
And hope 'neath flowers hid many a thorn,
  And made the prospect seem too bright;
And woeless tears bedew'd her eye —
The tears of heavenly ecstasy :—

And she was gazing on the light
  The star of evening round it shed,
As if it rose in glory bright
  To look upon her youthful head.
And, oh! she seem'd a fair young star
Gazing on kindred orbs afar.

Again I heard her pray when woe
  Had turn'd life's sweets to bitterness,
And Care had stamp'd upon her brow
  The seal of sorrow and distress;
And tho' no tear or sigh was there,
A thousand spoke in that short prayer.

Hope was not gone — 'twas still at strife
    With stern Despair for mastery ;
Still wreath'd the fading flowers of life —
    Still stifled down the bursting sigh ;
And fondly clung around the heart,
And, tho' it broke, would scarce depart.

I heard her pray when Hope was gone ;
    No earthly wish was in her prayer :
Her heart was wither'd and alone —
    Sunk in the calmness of despair.
That prayer for better worlds was given —
For Hope and Love had fled to Heaven.

And painless, pleasureless, were all
    The earthly feelings of her mind
And yet that prayer was musical
    As the low breath of Autumn wind,
That in the balmy evening breathes,
And sighs o'er summer's withering wreaths.

Once more I heard her pray: the last —

    Last tie to earth was breaking there:

And as she pray'd, her spirit pass'd,

    Wafted above by that pure prayer,

Like fading flowers that, as they die,

Breathe up to Heaven a fragrant sigh.

WRITTEN IN THE AUTHOR'S BIBLE,

THE DAY SHE COMPLETED HER FOURTEENTH YEAR.

Thou Book of Life ! thy healing balm still flows
To calm our grief — to ease our many woes.
Amid our trouble and adversity,
When mortal help hath fail'd, we turn to thee,
And find within thee never-failing truth —
A lamp to cheer our age and guide our youth.

The sailor wandering o'er the sea afar,
Deprived of light from every lesser star,
Upon the angry, stormy billows tost —
His vessel sinking, and his compass lost —

Oh, what bright hopes would fill his trembling soul,

If he should see the star that points the pole,

Over the foamy waves and billows dark

Shedding effulgence and etherial spark !

How would he steer his ship with grateful hand,

Led by that light, and guided safe to land?

So 'twas with me ; — tost on life's stormy wave,

I turn'd to thee, and found thee strong to save :

No longer o'er the sea of discord driven,

But safely harbour'd within sight of Heaven;

Lifted above the world's contentious strife,

And anchor'd by the Hope of bright Eternal Life.

THE TEAR.

Say what is that precious and beautiful drop,
   By sympathy render'd so dear—
Falling softly as dew on a flow'ret's top ? —
   That magical gem is a Tear.

When sorrow oppresses and sharpens her dart
   With her gloom and her doubt and her fear ; —
When she almost to breaking has loaded the heart,
   The relief of that heart is a Tear.

In Bethany, Lazarus sicken'd and died,
   And when the blest Saviour came near,
He look'd on the grave, and for pity he sigh'd —
   The Redeemer himself shed a Tear.

And when God shall call back the life he has given;

    In that hour of sorrow and fear,

May our penitent sighs waft us safely to Heaven,

    Our passport — a Penitent's Tear.

" WATCH AND PRAY."

Saw ye where the Saviour kept

Watch, while His disciples slept ?

Did ye hear that Saviour speak,

While the sweat bedew'd his cheek ?

Did ye listen to the Lord,

And receive the hallow'd word ?

Heard ye your Redeemer say

To his followers " Watch and pray ?"

Not to them alone that call : —

It was given alike for all —

All in pleasure, all in pain —

They that serve, and they that reign :

All alike are mortal dust ;

Vain is every earthly trust.

None can see how soon they may,

Be as nothing. — " Watch and pray !"

Rich men, in your palaces,

Where ye live in plenteous ease,

Glorying in your golden store,

Know ye not 'twill soon be o'er ! —

Have none told ye what must be,

That so careless still are ye ?

Hear it now — the voice obey :

Ye are mortal ! " Watch and pray !"

Maiden in thy beauty's pride,

With life's bitterness untried,

Know'st thou, tho' in life's young bloom,

Thou may'st perish in the tomb?

There the fairest flowers must wither —

Thou like them art hastening thither :

Beauty soon will pass away

Oh ! whilst lovely, " Watch and pray!"

Peasant, in thy lowly cot,

Murmuring at thy humble lot,

While thy children round thee strive,

Asking bread thou can'st not give, —

Wait with patience on the Lord ;

He will not forget his word :

Dark temptations strew thy way —

'Gainst their power " Watch and pray!"

Earthly wealth will not endure;

None 'gainst Time can be secure;

Rich, and poor, and king, and slave —

All must moulder in the grave!

But a day of wrath shall come:

·All again must quit the tomb.

See, it cometh!   Blest be they,

Who, while here, will " watch and pray."

THE END.

LONDON :
Printed by Littlewood and Green,
15, Old Bailey.

SD - #0086 - 210222 - C0 - 229/152/10 - PB - 9781331290414 - Gloss Lamination